THE SMART KID'S GUIDE TO

Manners

BY CHRISTINE PETERSEN • ILLUSTRATED BY RONNIE ROONEY

Published by The Child's World®
1980 Lookout Drive • Mankato, MN 56003-1705
800-599-READ • www.childsworld.com

Acknowledgments
The Child's World®: Mary Berendes, Publishing Director
Content Adviser: Philip C. Rodkin, Professor of Child
Development, Departments of Educational Psychology and
Psychology, University of Illinois
The Design Lab: Design
Red Line Editorial: Editorial Direction
Amnet: Production

Photographs © Shutterstock Images, cover, 1, 6, 7, 10, 12,
15, 16, 18, 19, 21, 25, 26, 27, 28, 29; Dmitry Naumov/
Shutterstock Images, 9; Aman Ahmed Khan/Shutterstock Images,
11; Veronica Louro/Shutterstock Images, 17; Konstantin Yolshin/
Shutterstock Images, 20; Antonio Diaz/Shutterstock Images, 23;
Tukaram Karve/Shutterstock Images, 24

ISBN 9781626873445
LCCN 2014930684

Printed in the United States of America
Mankato, MN
July, 2014
PA02224

ABOUT THE AUTHOR

Before becoming a freelance writer, Christine Petersen enjoyed diverse careers as a biologist and middle school science teacher. She has published more than 50 books for young people, covering topics in science, social studies, and health. Christine is a member of the Society of Children's Book Writers and Illustrators.

ABOUT THE ILLUSTRATOR

Ronnie Rooney took art classes constantly as a child. She was always drawing and painting at her mom's kitchen table. She got her BFA in painting from the University of Massachusetts at Amherst and her MFA in illustration from the Savannah College of Art and Design in Savannah, Georgia. Ronnie lives on a U.S. Army base with her infantryman husband and two small children. Ronnie hopes to pass on her love of art and sports to her kids.

CONTENTS

CHAPTER 1

What Are Manners?

George Washington was the first president of the
United States. He is one of the most important
people in American history. But George did not
grow up expecting to lead a nation. His father died
in 1743. George was 11. He was suddenly the oldest
man in his house. He could not travel to attend a
good school like wealthy boys his age. George had to
stay home and help his mother run the farm.

George studied at home when he could. He worked on more than math, reading, and writing. He knew it was also important to learn good **manners**. Manners are habits of kindness, respect, and honesty. They are the rules and customs that help people get along.

As a teenager, George Washington wrote down more than 100 manners rules in his journal. He used them for the rest of his life. George did not go to good schools. But he was **polite** and **respectful** of others. He became successful because people liked and respected him. Good manners helped him succeed.

George learned many rules about manners that are still important today. Here are a few from his little book that you should follow to be polite:

- Don't talk with your mouth full.
- Cover your cough, sneeze, or yawn.
- Be a good listener. Don't interrupt when others are speaking.
- Avoid cursing and other rude language.
- Never point or stare at others or whisper about them.

Rules for polite eating are different around the world.

Some manners have changed over time. Manners can also be different in other countries. Have you ever been told to stop making sounds while eating? There's no need to worry about that in Japan. Slurping your noodles shows a Japanese cook that you like the food. Many American kids are expected to keep their arms off the table. Children in Europe learn just the opposite. Their families think it is bad manners to hide hands under the table.

Why are manners so important when they can change over time and from place to place? Good manners help people get along wherever they live.

You don't need to learn 100 manners rules by heart like George Washington did. Good manners can be simple if you remember the Golden Rule. Always treat others as you wish to be treated. People feel good when you are kind to them. They notice when you show respect. When you are honest, others feel they can trust you. That goodness will be returned to you in many ways throughout your life.

Sharing is one of the first manners young children are expected to learn. When you share, you take turns or use something together. That sounds easy. But it can feel like you are losing something. Remember  that sharing goes both ways. Share with someone, and they are more likely to share with you in return. That can be fun!

CHAPTER 2

Why Do We Need Manners?

Manners can seem hard if you think of them as rules. But when it comes to manners, the details are less important than the big picture. It does not matter if you use the wrong fork at dinner. You can sometimes forget to shake an adult's hand when you meet him or her. No one knows exactly how to behave in every situation. The important thing is to treat others with kindness, respect, and honesty.

Some people think manners are old-fashioned. It is never out of style to be thoughtful. Think of all the people you see in one week. You have family at home. At school, you work with dozens of other children. Perhaps you also play a sport or take a class after school. Your list should also include the people you pass on shopping trips and at restaurants. And don't forget your friends! Manners help you and everyone else get along.

How can you help the people around you?

Try to stay positive!

You may have heard a coach or teacher say that **attitude** is catching. That means one person's mood can affect others. It might go like this. Someone is mean to you, and it ruins your day. You snap at a friend. He or she plays with someone else. At home, you fuss about doing your chores. Now your friends and family are feeling bad, too. The pattern continues until someone stops it. It's hard to have good manners when others make bad choices. Remember that a positive attitude is catching, too.

Scientists have watched what happens when someone is treated kindly. The person's brain begins to produce a special chemical. The chemical causes that person to want to be kind in return. It proves that you really can change someone's attitude. All it takes is a smile, hello, or thank-you. Imagine that! Your good manners can start a chain reaction of happiness.

You can do the right thing even when you're by yourself.

People sometimes think we don't need manners when no one is looking. Actually, that is when they matter most of all! Good manners help us make the right decisions when there is no one to tell us what to do. You won't get a gold star or high five at such moments. Instead, you feel self-respect. You can see yourself as a good person.

Here's a small example. You are supposed to join a friend at the park in a few minutes. Rolling your bike out of the garage, you notice that it has a flat tire. Hmm. Your sister isn't home. Maybe you could ride her bicycle! Good manners remind you not to use another person's things without asking. What if you damaged the bike by accident? You can still walk to the park or call your friend to make other plans.

Follow the Golden Rule to solve problems like this. Think about how your actions affect other people. Treat them how you wish to be treated. You will feel happier and stronger when you make good choices.

CHAPTER 3

Building Strong Manners

Good manners require you to be patient even when you are feeling sad, tired, or worried. Sometimes you must be polite when others hurt your feelings. It takes time to learn these skills.

You might run every day to build strong legs and lungs. **Self-control** is a kind of inner strength.

You can also build it with practice. Self-control helps you think before you act. Take a deep breath when you are upset. Think how you would like to be treated, and show that same respect to other people. These actions will become habits.

Self-control and manners work together. See if you can imagine how self-control and manners would help in the situations in this chapter.

It's okay to stop and think before you react to something.

Does your family have rules about using phones and electronics?

Your family goes out to dinner. Your brother has a new game on his phone. He plays instead of talking with the family. Then he offers you a turn. What do you do?

A new game is hard to resist. But phones and other electronics are disturbing in public places. Many families have rules about not using phones at the table, too. Thank your brother for offering to let you play. Ask him if you can try it later at home. Suggest that your brother turn the phone off so your family can talk instead. Other diners will respect your thoughtfulness, too.

The bell has just rung for recess. All morning, you've looked forward to playing basketball with your best friends. You run out to the playground. Just as you reach the sports equipment, another student pushes past you and grabs the last basketball. What do you do?

Your feelings might be hurt when someone pushes you. You might become angry. But it will not help to shove back. Try speaking politely to the other child. Ask if you can use the basketball when he is done with it. You could also walk calmly away and play another game with your friends. It is important to have good manners even when others are rude. Friends and adults notice when you make good choices. It shows that you are a leader.

Try to stay calm even when others won't share.

Being part of a team feels good, even if you lose the game.

A new player has joined your soccer team. He doesn't have much experience. Your teammates get mad when he misses a pass. They ignore him after the game.

It is disappointing to lose a game when you have practiced so much. It is also hard to disagree with your friends. But think back to when you started playing a new sport. You probably made some mistakes, too. Everyone deserves a chance to feel like part of the team, even if they never become the star.

You could offer to practice with your new teammate to build his skills. You might wind up making a great new friend.

Have you ever seen someone get mad when they lose a game? Maybe they blamed someone else for the loss. That person was being a poor sport. Good sports can show respect when others win. They understand that winning is great, but it is not the most important thing. They know treating people with respect and kindness is more important. When you lose, you can learn from mistakes and practice to get better. You are a good sport when you focus on teamwork and fun instead of winning.

A hug and an apology can help make things better.

Your mother finds that there is a crack in her favorite coffee mug. You put away dishes the night before. She yells at you for breaking the mug. What do you do?

Your mom probably overreacted by yelling. But you can still behave with good manners. You can earn trust by admitting when you make a mistake. "I'm sorry" can heal the wounds when you damage someone's belongings or hurt their feelings. Offer to help fix the mug. If it can't be repaired, just give her a hug. Saying "I'm sorry that I broke your mug" shows that you care about your mother's feelings.

You can learn manners by watching adults and older children. How do they **interact** with each other? Notice what happens when a person is treated **rudely**. What is the difference if someone is kind to them? Good manners help people trust each other.

Watch how adults are polite to each other.

CHAPTER 4
Good Manners Are a Choice

You have seen some situations in which good manners can prevent or solve problems. Here are the **principles** of good manners. You can use them in your everyday life.

Show that you are thankful. It is always good to send a card after someone gives you a gift.

It doesn't matter whether or not you like it. Find something nice to say about the gift or the person who gave it. Thankfulness is important at other times, too. Your family, teachers, and friends make your life better with the things they do. Let them know you appreciate the effort. Surprise them now and then by simply saying thank you.

Show thanks when people do nice things for you.

Telling secrets can make people feel bad.

Think before you speak. Just as "thank you" makes people smile, some words can hurt. A person feels sad and alone when disrespected. **Gossip** can ruin friendships and get people in trouble. Even normal words can start an argument when they are spoken impatiently. Think twice before you say something that might be hurtful. Add "please" when you make a request for help. Use "excuse me" when your actions disturb others. You will find that these words really do work magic in helping you get along with others.

Listen to others. Everyone wants a turn to speak. But imagine the chaos if no one ever listened! Your teacher could never complete a lesson if the students talked instead of paying attention. The coach could not show you a new skill, and you'd be sitting around instead of playing. You wouldn't be able to understand the story of a television show if all the characters were talking at once. Everyone has different ideas. You won't agree with all of them. But listening helps us learn.

Wait patiently in line for your turn, too.

Practice your sharing skills!

Respect belongings. How does it feel when someone uses your things without asking? Sometimes this might not bother you. Other times it probably bothers you a lot. Ask before you use someone else's stuff. Be especially thoughtful when you visit friends or family members. When you have permission to borrow something, use it carefully. Try not to break it or wear it out.

Respect privacy. Sometimes people need **privacy**. It's important to knock if you want to open a closed door. Someone on the other side might want to be alone. Respect others' privacy when you are asking questions, too. It is okay to ask polite questions as you get to know someone. You just don't want to seem nosy.

Always knock before you go through a closed door.

You can choose to be helpful. That's good manners, too!

Help out. There is always work to do. Look around and see how you can help. Your parents will thank you for pitching in around the house. Did you make a mess in the lunchroom at school? Grab some paper towels and wipe it up. Before you leave a friend's house, you can pick up the toys you used. It is always good manners to clean up your messes.

You can't control how other people behave. But you can control how you react. You make a choice every time you use good manners. It is a choice that shows you care about others as well as yourself.

Think back to the last argument you had. Most arguments happen because people want to be right. They want to win. But there are usually no real winners in an argument. Instead, people just get angrier. Try listening instead of fighting. Good manners can help people solve problems.

TOP TEN THINGS TO KNOW

1. It's hard to have good manners when others make bad choices.
2. Good manners help people get along.
3. Manners are habits of kindness, respect, and honesty.
4. Good manners help you make positive choices in life.
5. Each country, community, and culture has some different ideas about good manners.
6. Manners grow stronger with practice.
7. The Golden Rule works everywhere. Treat others as you wish to be treated.
8. Everyone benefits when people use good manners.
9. Good manners are important every day, in every situation.
10. Good manners show that you respect yourself and other people.

GLOSSARY

attitude (AT-i-tood) Attitude is how one feels, thinks, or behaves. Try to keep a good attitude in difficult situations.

gossip (GAH-sip) Gossip is talk about other people's business. Gossip can hurt other people's feelings.

interact (intur-AKT) To interact is to have an effect on someone or something else. Be polite when you interact with other people.

manners (MAN-urs) Manners are habits of kindness, respect, and honesty that help people get along. Good manners sometimes take practice.

polite (puh-LITE) People who are polite are thoughtful and show good manners. A polite person is well behaved.

principles (PRIN-suh-puhls) Principles are important beliefs or truths. There are several principles of good manners.

privacy (PRYE-vuh-see) Privacy is the state of being alone or having a place that is not shared with others. You should respect other people's privacy.

respectful (ri-SPEKT-ful) Being respectful is showing you care about others as much as yourself. Good manners help you be respectful of others.

rudely (ROOD-ly) Behaving rudely is acting in a way that is unkind or thoughtless. Try to not act rudely at school.

self-control (SELF-kohn-TROHL) Self-control is the ability to manage your own behavior. You can practice your self-control like any other skill.

BOOKS

Berenstain, Jan and Mike. *The Berenstain Bears Say Please and Thank You.* New York: Harper, 2011.

Marsico, Katie. *Taking Turns!* Ann Arbor, MI: Cherry Lake Publishing, 2013.

Raatma, Lucia. *Good Manners.* New York: Children's Press, 2013.

WEB SITES

Visit our Web site for links about manners:
childsworld.com/links

Note to Parents, Teachers, and Librarians:
We routinely verify our Web links to make sure they are safe and active sites. So encourage your readers to check them out!

INDEX